10 STEPS TO MANAGING CHANGE IN SCHOOLS

How do we take initiatives from goals to actions?

Jeffrey
BENSON

ASCD Alexandria, VA USA

Website: www.ascd.org   www.ascdarias.org
E-mail: books@ascd.org

PAPERBACK ISBN: 978-1-4166-2132-4   ASCD product # SF115072

Also available as an e-book (see Books in Print for the ISBNs).

Library of Congress Cataloging-in-Publication Data
Benson, Jeffrey.
10 steps to managing change in schools : how do we take initiatives from goals to actions? / Jeffrey Benson.
    pages cm
 Includes bibliographical references.
  ISBN 978-1-4166-2132-4 (pbk. : alk. paper) 1. Educational planning. 2. Educational change. 3. Educational leadership. 4. School improvement programs. I. Title. II. Title: Ten steps to managing change in schools.
  LC71.2.B46 2015
  371.2'07--dc23   2015024912

24 23 22 21 20 19 18 17 16 15   1 2 3 4 5 6 7 8 9 10

10 STEPS TO MANAGING CHANGE IN SCHOOLS

How do we take initiatives from goals to actions?

Want to earn a free ASCD Arias e-book?
Your opinion counts! Please take 2–3 minutes to give
us your feedback on this publication. All survey
respondents will be entered into a drawing to
win an ASCD Arias e-book.

Please visit
www.ascd.org/ariasfeedback

Thank you!

Introduction

In my work as a consultant and workshop presenter, I help schools and districts improve their program initiatives. Over the years, I've helped educators find ways to hold more effective IEP meetings, help staff work better as a team, increase the use of authentic assessments, use literature for developing social skills, and any number of other objectives. Unfortunately, even when teachers and administrators give me high marks, I find that any changes I may have helped to bring about are rarely robust and lasting. Although workshops and presentations provide schools with a common language, inspiration, and skills, these are too often adopted piecemeal and at *random* by educators who don't have a set approach to implementing change. In the pages that follow, I offer a change model that can be successfully adapted to almost all program initiatives, so you don't have to exert time and energy to reinvent the wheel with every new improvement campaign.

Reality is never as predictable as we might think. Formulas exist in the absence of emotions, uncertainties, and shifting forces. As a mentor of mine once put it, "Be nimble in your leadership." By the same token, I would encourage you to be nimble in adapting to your circumstances the model I offer here. Use it as a touchstone, not as a millstone. Remember that change is a process, not an event; it's never completely "done." You will have many opportunities to identify and celebrate successes big and small. There will come a time when your change initiative is no longer the focus of your energies and resources—at which point you can begin the process of implementing another improvement campaign. .

All administrators are middle managers, with authority over some people and under the scrutiny and authority of others—a reality that my model takes into account. I share the conventional wisdom that empowering staff and students benefits schools, and that a dynamic leadership team is critical to a school's success. In the pages that follow, I use the pronoun "you" when referring to school leadership to mean a single administrator or a leadership team. The authority granted to you by the organizational hierarchy is an invaluable resource towards meeting your school's mission. My change model should help you to use that authority thoroughly and wisely.

Step 1: Understand the Catalysts for Change

There are three general catalysts for school change:

1. Regulatory directives. These demands come every year. Some have very high stakes and must be accomplished in what seems like an unreasonably short time. Though you may be angry and overwhelmed, you are still responsible for rallying your team to do the work well.

2. A crisis that exposes a problem. A break-in reveals how poorly the school is secured each evening, your students' subpar standardized test scores are published in the local newspaper, a group of prominent students cheat on an important exam: In each of these cases, everyone looks to you for direction.

3. A need or desire for improvement is identified. There are always elements of the school that can improve if given sustained attention, and stakeholders—leaders, teachers, students, parents, and members of the community—may bring a particular area into focus. You probably don't have the time or the resources to improve everything at once, but sometimes conditions may allow you to choose one area for robust improvement.

Good school leadership requires you to prioritize opportunities for change.

Change is hard, and people vary in their capacity to handle it. They also vary in their perceptions of what risks are worth taking—though there are always risks to both leaving the status quo as it is and taking action to implement change. Risk raises fears, which can in turn distort an objective analysis of a given situation. The following questionnaire is intended to help you avoid such distortion and to ensure that you neither overlook areas in need of change or jump to fix areas that should not be a priority.

Risk-Assessment Questionnaire for Change

1. What category of change is under consideration?

    A. A regulatory directive

    B. A crisis

    C. A need for improvement

2. If you answered "C" above, who identified the need for improvement? How many people have expressed concern? To what degree do the number of people expressing concern and their levels of influence matter in deciding whether to take action?

3. What might happen if you choose not to invest in a large change initiative? Articulate a number of possibilities.

4. How likely is it that any of the possibilities you answered for the above question will happen? This is not a call for a deep mathematical analysis based on an extensive review of the available research. Consider the probability based on your available experience and expertise:

    A. Inevitable

    B. Very likely

    C. Moderately likely

    D. Unlikely

    E. Very unlikely

5. If one of the outcomes you listed were to happen, could the basic procedures that you've currently got in place

handle the impact? If so, you might not need to invest the resources of a schoolwide change campaign.

6. Has the ground shifted at your school so that change is now required? If so, how much change do you think your school can tolerate?

7. What inspiring vision can drive the school change initiative? As an educator once told me, "Leaders are managers of optimism and inspiration." Risk, though often necessary, is something most educators prefer to avoid. Remember that a positive sense of the future sustains effort. Positive emotions drive change forward; negative ones land it in a ditch. Develop a positive vision of change and convey a sense of sincere emotional optimism. Put that vision into words and make it the headline of your change campaign.

Here is an example of how leaders might fill out the above questionnaire:

1. *Answer:* C. A need for improvement. We are examining whether to implement a school change initiative for our math program to improve outcomes. Five years ago, we set our sights on improving writing across the curriculum. By all accounts, our writing program is a success. Our math program, however, is not doing as well. The math department chair has stepped up to discuss this, and the leadership has noted the stagnant test scores the past three years.

2. *Answer:* The math team has some strong teachers and the department chair is a school leader, so their concerns should carry weight.

3. *Answer:* If we don't achieve better math scores our self-confidence and sense of purpose will erode. When leaders don't lead, people notice. Our math teachers might end up seeking employment elsewhere; there is a new charter school opening nearby, dedicated to math and science. Our school will be vulnerable to the loss of families who highly value math.

4. *Answer:* C. Moderately likely. The stagnant scores are not a crisis, but they should be on our radar. If the scores dip, public trust in our school will follow. Math teachers may not be likely to leave our school under current conditions, but the department chair has been approached by the local university, and it is possible that she would leave if she felt her concerns were being ignored. If she were to leave, the faculty would be weakened, and the community might begin to see the local charter school as a preferable alternative. Such a perception could cause us to lose significant number of our best students.

5. *Answer:* We would be able to manage any one of the possible outcomes if they happened in isolation, but in this case they're intertwined.

6. *Answer:* The opening of the math-focused charter school nearby has clearly shifted the ground for us. We believe our school leaders should take action while problems are still manageable and not yet at a crisis level.

7. *Answer:* We have articulated our positive visions as follows: Our school will have an outstanding, universally praised math program that helps make our school the pride of the community!

Step 2: Clarify Positions and Interests

Ms. A. tells me that she's angry because the new principal has asked her to move a pile of ragged boxes from the entrance to her class. She says it's not a safety or fire hazard, she likes the boxes where they are, and she doesn't think the principal should be micromanaging her. I suggest that she ask the principal what purpose he thinks moving the boxes will serve, and she agrees.

When Ms. A. meets the principal, he explains to her that the school is initiating a campaign to improve executive functioning—an issue dear to Ms. A's heart. He tells Ms. A.

that he doesn't think her pile of boxes conveys the right message, but he also apologizes for not explaining himself sooner.

"I share your goal of presenting an organized appearance," responds Ms. A. "I have a pretty Mexican blanket that would fit nicely over those boxes."

The principal says he thinks that's a great solution. The boxes don't end up moving, but the entrance to Ms. A's room now looks much better.

Positions vs. Interests

The language of positions and interests (Fischer & Uri, 1981) allows us to make sense of all school activity, but none more so than implementation of a change initiative. The principal's request that Ms. A. move her boxes was a position— a specific strategy. When we present only our position but not our interests, we compromise the creativity and shared ownership essential to moving forward together as a community. By stating only his position, the principal set up a win-lose, my-way-or-the-highway conflict; it was only by articulating his interests—the elements that are driving his position—in this case a well-organized environment—that the principal was able to work with Ms. A. to craft options agreeable to both.

Schools are full of people who state their positions without making their interests known: a student asks to sit next to a friend, a teacher requests a schedule change, parents ask for their children to retake a test, the receptionist wants a new filing cabinet. All of these are positions, but what are the interests that individuals are trying to meet with their requests? You may not agree with the position—for example, you may not think the school can afford a new filing cabinet—but you may share the interests that the position is trying to meet (you also don't want the receptionist to have to wrestle with a dysfunctional file drawer every day). Perhaps the solution is to ask the janitor to take 15 minutes to fix the drawer. But you can't join in crafting more strategies without knowing the interests driving the initial requests.

Most significant interests in schools are shared: we all want students to learn, be resilient, and be good citizens. One reason many mission statements have little effect on outcomes is that educators don't persistently refer back to them as though they reflect the school community's deepest shared interests—and when they do reference them, it's often to force a single strategy or position into action ("Because safety is one of our most cherished interests, everyone therefore must . . ."). Change initiatives are most likely to take root in organizations where people are consistently leading with their interests and inviting multiple strategies to meet them.

By invoking the school's deepest shared interests, you allow staff to bring passion to and claim ownership of the change initiative. The more people are creatively and enthusiastically empowered to make your school's interests come alive, the likelier it is that your school will live up to its mission statement. Just remember to start with interests—positions can come later. The steps in the following checklist will help you to ensure that your change initiative is both strongly rooted in shared interests and focused on meeting them.

Checklist for Meeting Shared Interests through Change

1. Confirm that your school's "inspired vision" (see Question 7 of the Risk Assessment Questionnaire for Change) reflects only interests and not positions.

2. Explain how the goals of your change initiative reflect the interests of your school's vision and mission statements.

The above two initial steps should raise positive emotions among staff. It's exciting to move forward on deeply shared interests—after all, it's what brought us into the profession in the first place. However, the next steps are likely to require deeper consideration into the depth and breadth of your commitment to your interests. Your school probably doesn't have the resources to fully address every competing interest related to the change initiative, so it's vital that you prioritize among them.

The following steps are also recursive: you need to revisit them at various times as you implement your change initiative.

3. List any interests related to the change initiative that may only be implied in your school's mission statement. (For example, the interest of being in regulatory compliance is

rarely referenced in any school's mission statement, yet it could well be critical to a change initiative.)

4. Given all you have to do as a school, prioritize the interests that you feel you can rally your staff around and that are likely to remain most important as the initiative unfolds. Being able to identify three important interests is a good benchmark (one is not enough to generate passion and creativity, and more than three risks diluting your focus).

5. Clearly articulate the interests of your change initiative, underscoring its relationship to the school's mission.

Here is how the leaders of our hypothetical school might complete the steps in the checklist:

1. Our school's inspired vision is reflected in our mission statement, which exhorts us to "develop capable, confident life-long learners who contribute to their community, participate thoughtfully in democracy, and succeed in a diverse and evolving global society. "The interests we seek to meet with our change initiative include having skilled and inspired math students, supporting teachers in developing a robust math program, engendering pride in our accomplishments when we work together, understanding and improving how we manage the change process, performing beyond the standards, minimizing flight to the charter school, and retaining our strongest teachers.

2. A key component of our mission is creating lifelong learners, and our robust math program will include the types of projects that allow students to make connections between school work and the world beyond. Supporting math teachers as they develop the math program allows them to model lifelong learning for students.

3. Though not specifically mentioned in our mission statement, engendering pride in our accomplishments is an interest central to our change initiative. We believe that a sense of pride in math accomplishments helps to build confidence and a willingness to handle the work of our diverse global society.

4. The three interests most critical to our change initiative are (1) having skilled and inspired math students, (2) supporting teachers in developing a robust math program, and (3) engendering pride in our accomplishments.

5. We will have a universally praised, outstanding math program that inspires students, supports the role teachers play in shaping our school, and helps make our school the pride of the community for what we accomplish as a team.

Step 3: Turn Interests into Targets

School change initiatives give us a chance to switch gears— to say proudly, "This is what we are going to accomplish that is new, different, and improved!" Our work in Step 3 is to find identifiable targets for your school change initiatives that are tangible. We get into the specifics, with our interests close at hand. To this end, I recommend completing a task analysis of the change initiative. There are two separate components to a successful task analysis: (1) breaking the task down into its many separate parts and (2) identifying those that require the most attention. Good teachers already do this: for example, when students fail to complete their homework, teachers might first consider all the possible reasons (e.g., trouble understanding the work, too many assignments, interference from after-school hobbies and jobs, family problems) and use their knowledge and judgement to prioritize their focus.

Task Analysis Checklist

The Task Analysis Checklist will help you to break down your change initiative into components that can serve as benchmarks of progress. By completing the checklist and revisiting it periodically, you will be able to identify specific targets that provide you with evidence of early success:

1. Write down your vision of change, being sure to align it with your school's mission statement.

2. List the activities and functions that your change initiative seeks to improve. What actions will students be taking to make this happen? What about teachers and administrators? Parents? What will you see and hear in the school community?

3. Identify three changes from Step 2 of this checklist that you believe will have a significant effect on the ultimate success of the change initiative. These three items will become your primary targets and serve as short-term benchmarks of the initiative's success.

Here is how the leaders of our hypothetical school might complete the steps in the Task Analysis Checklist:

1. Our vision for change is as follows: "We will have an outstanding and universally praised math program that inspires students, supports the role that teachers play in shaping our school, and helps make our school the pride of the community for what we accomplish as a team.

2. We expect to see the following changes as a result of our initiative:

> • More students signing up for non-required math courses

- Higher scores on standardized tests
- More students contributing math projects to our academic fair
- Teachers suggesting new math electives
- More interdisciplinary projects related to math
- Interesting math posters and displays in the school
- Notes of appreciation for parents and guardians
- More students accepted to competitive colleges
- Math teachers leading in-service workshops
- Fewer students complaining that they're not good at math

3. Our three primary targets are as follows:

- More students signing up for non-required math courses
- Higher scores on standardized tests
- More interdisciplinary projects related to math

Step 4: Seize Control of Data

I worked for years in special education settings with very challenging students who struggled constantly in their idio-syncratic journeys towards stability. The schools in which I worked had very good reputations; looking back at the accomplishments of our students, their families, and staff, I feel a great sense of satisfaction and pride. We made a difference in so many ways, yet we were lax in cataloging those differences—a common oversight in many special education programs. As the focus of our national agenda for child development shifted to standardized testing, the accomplishments of special education programs became more and more hard to discern, like mists dispersed by a strong wind. We in the special education community failed to own and embrace data that mattered to us, and that would have mattered to others.

The climate of data is driven by those who demand it. Because so many school reform initiatives are directed from central and distant offices, many schools struggle to develop a sense of ownership over data. Instead, teachers perceive the gathering of data as an interruption of their work.

Your change initiative is a great opportunity to seize control of data that matter to you. Schools are overflowing with information that can be creatively gathered and used to improve conditions. By gathering and analyzing data for themselves, school staff can cultivate a renewed sense of purpose, highlight meaningful accomplishments, and identify benchmarks around which to rally. It is critically important for the long-term success of your initiative that everyone can see progress happening—positive energy grows exponentially from the evidence that your school community's efforts are making a difference. Because change initiatives usually take a long time to implement fully, data serve as tools in your role as a manager of optimism.

In Step 3, you were asked to identify three tasks to serve as benchmarks of progress for your change initiative. These three targets link the work you are doing both to the specific interests of the initiative and to the lofty goals of your mission statement. Gathering and disseminating data around your three main benchmarks allows for chances to rally, recommit to change, and can calm concerns that the efforts might not be worth the disruption to the status quo. If you aspire to lofty goals, you need to be stepping up on solid evidence as you ascend to great heights. Use the following Data Gathering Checklist to ensure that the information you collect is aligned to your vision of change.

Data Collection Checklist

With the three benchmarks from Step 3 in mind, answer the questions in this checklist. Remember that you want data to be unambiguous, easy to gather, and invigorating for the school community.

1. Consider potentially relevant *institutional data.* Among the types of data readily available in most school record-keeping systems are attendance information, standardized tests scores, referrals to the school and to school programs, staff retention information, budget expenditures, formal parent complaints, and critical incidence reports.

2. Consider potentially relevant *uncollected data.* These are data that are gathered ad-hoc rather than as a matter of course. Examples include information about the number of students who participate in community service, community members who attend school events, cooperative learning moments during classroom walkthroughs, discussions with parents, and hours devoted to scoring tests.

Although gathering uncollected data can raise everyone's interest in your change initiative, it can also take time away from other responsibilities, so it is important to streamline the procedures involved. Recall the language of positions and interests: If you approach your team only with demands and glancing references to goals, you will not soothe their concerns or promote their creative involvement. Always lead with interests ("Our interests are to keep track of the number of students who complete their homework and to not overburden teachers in the process. What are all the ways we can meet these interests?")

3. Consider potentially relevant sources of *isolated data*. These are sources of data that often go unrecognized. Examples include satisfaction surveys, which can provide useful information about community emotions and perceptions (many of which are readily available online); time studies (e.g., how long it takes to get everyone fed at lunch); and reviews of the school's physical condition, which are easy to administer and can involve a variety of stakeholders.

4. Prioritize your data-collection options. Balance accuracy with available resources and opportunity to build momentum with ease of use. There are no perfect surveys, and all data can be corrupted and manipulated, but prioritization is useful and necessary. Remember that what you choose to focus on will have a powerful effect on the school community and set in motion the process of change.

Collecting baseline data for the three main benchmarks of your initiative may require a variety of approaches. Perhaps you've identified a benchmark that defies any reasonable form of measurement; if that's the case, go back and find another one. The data that you gather and analyze will not determine whether change will happen; you have already made that decision. Rather, the data serve to gauge present conditions, much like an oil dipstick or a thermometer.

Keep in mind the following construct: Data lead to information leads to knowledge leads to wisdom. In the context of a change initiative,

- *Data* refers to raw numbers ("23 teachers were surveyed and 17 of them did not get their entire prep period today").
- *Information* refers to an orderly accounting of the data in subjective terms that reveal an underlying condition ("An overwhelming majority of the teachers did not get their entire prep period today").
- *Knowledge* refers subjectively to the underlying condition as one that needs addressing ("There is a problem with protecting teacher prep periods").
- *Wisdom* refers to an informed course of action for putting the knowledge to use in improving the underlying condition ("We have to look again at the number of meetings we are asking teachers to attend every day if we want to assure that prep periods are protected").

In addition to exposing areas for improvement, data provide you with a powerful opportunity to acknowledge the ways in which your school is already manifesting best practices and the staff members who can serve as models for change. Your initiative will only be as strong as your belief in your collective abilities, and your fellow practitioners may already be doing some of what it takes to make the initiative successful.

Data provide us with a powerful opportunity to acknowledge what is going well and to identify what Heath and Heath (2010) call "bright spots": the areas in which your school is already manifesting best practices, and the educators who are modeling those practices best. You will build your initiative with your strengths and a belief in your collective abilities, and solid practitioners at your school may already be doing some of what it takes. (In Step 5, your bright spots will find their place in the plan you are building.)

Here is how the leaders of our hypothetical school might complete the steps in the Data Collection Checklist:

1. Potentially relevant institutional data:

- High-stakes test and SAT scores
- Enrollment numbers for non-required math courses
- Grade distribution among math classes

2. Potentially relevant uncollected data:

- Categories of projects at the academic fair

- Number of students signing up for multiple math courses
- Number of students with low standardized test scores in math taking math-based electives

3. Potentially relevant sources of isolated data:

- A survey of the prerequisite skills that students think they need to sign up for math electives
- A survey of parents' knowledge about and attitudes toward math electives

4. After a lively discussion, our team has chosen not to focus on test scores for now, as we believe that they are already bound to rise if we attend to other features of the math program that teachers find more engaging. Instead, we have decided to focus our attention on the number of students enrolled in non-required math classes. Any increase in enrollment will suggest that we are making progress toward our vision for change and will be a particularly significant benchmark after the charter school opens nearby, as it will prove our capacity to compete directly with it. The team was intrigued by the possibility of tracking how many of our lower-achieving math students were still taking math-based electives—a healthy number would suggest a shift in student attitudes—but ultimately didn't feel that the relevant data would be robust enough to be worth the effort of collecting it.

Step 5: Build a Force Field

Our capacity to make wise decisions is complicated by the endless unpredictability of human beings. One ineffective way in which we deal with such complexity is by ignoring information that we can't easily understand and jump into action. When you are leading a school change initiative, you don't just jump into action: the consequences of failure are significant, and you can't possibly know everything there is to know. A force field analysis allows your team to sit with the complexity of the real world before deciding on actions in a way that

- Provides for abundant and diverse input,
- Brings to light conflicting opinions,
- Compels the team to assess existing strengths that are necessary for success,
- Produces positive energy, and
- Counteracts the enervating idea that the team is somehow starting from scratch. (Remember, there are always bright spots!)

The first step in creating a force field is to set up a large piece of paper with the issue that you wish to consider written at the very top. Directly below it, write "Ideal Situation," and at the bottom of the page write "Absolute Worst Situation." A horizontal line running between the top and bottom text represents your current status. The team must ask: "If the bottom of the page is the condition of having nothing at all in our favor, and the top of the page is the condition of everything being perfect and us having nothing left to accomplish, where shall we place the line that represents our current status?" (See Figure 1 for a force field template.)

FIGURE: 1 **Force Field Template**

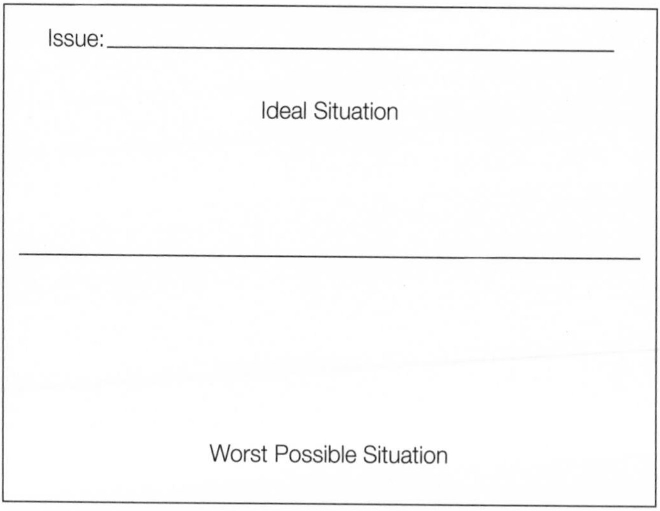

Issue: _____

Ideal Situation

_____

Worst Possible Situation

Next, the team must determine the *driving* forces pushing the school *up* toward its goal and the *restraining* forces that are pushing the school *down* from an ideal state. These forces are represented by arrows pointing up and down from the horizontal line, the length and width of which represent the relative strength the team assigns to each force.

Figure 2 shows an example of a force field that our hypothetical school team constructed to address one aspect of

FIGURE 2: **Student Enrollment in Non-Required Math Courses**

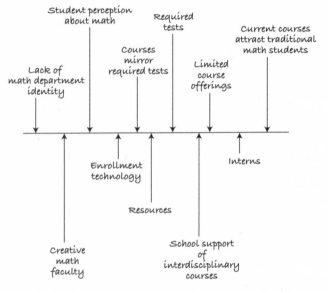

Ideal Situation—every student enrolls in non-required math courses

Absolute Worst Situation—no students enroll in non-required math courses

its change initiative. (You may wish to begin with a force field analysis of the entire initiative first before creating ones for discrete components.) The force field diagram should remain in everyone's view throughout the process of analysis so that everyone can refer to it.

Force field analysis is a messy, opinionated, and creative exercise, and responses do not have to emerge in any order. Some forces may be both restraining *and* driving; in such cases, have them point in both directions, with comments attached to clarify. You may find it helpful to break forces down into the following categories:

- Staff skills
- Student skills
- School resources
- Community resources
- Parent involvement
- Regulatory imperatives
- Emotions
- Impact of social media
- School traditions
- Rules and policies

When the team has stopped generating input, the team leader should explicitly ask: "Are we done? Is anyone considering anything else that hasn't already been represented?"

Force Field Analysis Checklist

1. Assemble a diverse team. You want your force field to be informed by as many perspectives as possible, because the success of your initiative depends on being able to develop a complex understanding of all the forces at work maintaining the status quo. None of the forces you identify exist in isolation—they are all woven together, often through subtle threads in the community.

2. Make sure everyone has a clear view of the force field. Describe the process in easily understood terms. Show team members an example of a completed force field, such as the one in Figure 1.

3. Don't split hairs about the placement of the initial horizontal line. If there isn't a clear consensus, say, "I think we can draw the line about 40 percent of the way up the page to get us started. What we all agree is that we have work to do. The next steps will take us there."

4. Solicit opinions on the sizes of the arrows. Begin by choosing an obvious force to put in place on the line that can serve as a guide for the relative sizes of the others. Don't worry too much about how wide or narrow the arrows are; note the difference opinions, but remember that your main interest is to place the forces in the diagram so that they aren't overlooked.

5. Save the diagram. Your force field will be a touchstone both for shared understanding and for assessing progress as the initiative evolves.

Step 6: Frame Your Efforts

One of the first and hardest lessons for teachers to learn is that they don't actually control their students—they can control all of the classroom elements that *influence* their students, from the arrangement of desks to the pacing of lessons to the tone of the teachers' voices. By maximizing the degree to which they can influence and organize these elements, teachers can develop a classroom environment in which students are well positioned to grow. Michal Fullan (2001) reminds us that "change . . . can be understood and perhaps led, but it cannot be controlled." You may not control the scores of people walking into your school every day, but you have a tremendous capacity to influence the environment in which those people make decisions and take actions.

You set and monitor the conditions within which your school will develop its change initiative. If you want to create change that will last, you must identify the elements of the environment that you can most successfully influence. Put another way: *you must identify ways to disturb the status quo of your force field.* Here are some elements of your school that you might consider altering for this purpose:

- Schedules
- Rules
- Internal procedures
- Modes of official communication
- Staff meeting agendas
- Placement of informational bulletin boards and plaques
- Composition of school committees
- Expectations for working with challenging students

Bolman and Deal (1984) identify the following four frames to consider when evaluating elements of your change initiative:

1. Structural. Rules, procedures, schedules, and job definitions are the bricks and mortars of your school. Reliability, predictability, efficiency, and accountability are essential to the success of the structural elements in your force field. If your school is a machine, then the structural elements are the central gears and parts.

2. Human Resources. This frame refers to the ways in which people affiliate, support, motivate, and provide one another with opportunities for growth. School leaders influence the force field by building trust, safety, partnerships, and belonging. At the top administrative levels, securing benefits, raises, and professional development opportunities are central elements. Initiatives that improve person-to-person understanding, learning, and communication can be powerfully disruptive to your force field. Giving an extra pat on the back to the bright spots who are helping your school to succeed and allowing them to train others is one way of working within a human resources frame. Leaders motivate the school community to fulfill the change initiative by expressing their belief in the power of human connection to overcome many of the challenges in our complex world.

3. Symbolic. The beliefs that staff, students, and families share about "how we do things around here" are the cornerstone of the symbolic frame. What we prioritize on our agendas, what we spend money on, what we send memos about, and whom and what we praise continually convey what what is important. Meetings are as much about symbolism as they are about content—they are ways for us to communicate what matters to us as a community. How you talk to difficult parents in the hallway or extol the successes at your school—these elements are squarely in the symbolic frame. School leaders are always working in the symbolic frame. If we think of schools as theaters, symbolic frames allow us to conceive of our work as a continuing drama from which people take meaning.

4. Power and politics. There's an old saying: "If you don't play politics, it plays you." Power and politics, like conflicts and diversity of opinion, are inevitable in schools. Your willingness to engage with these combustible elements for the sake of a successful change initiative puts you in this frame. Develop the voices of those who can influence the team. Consciously engage supporters and build cohorts to support initiatives. Increase the authority of your bright spots. Listen to those who are not in your corner so that they can be heard. In the power and politics frame, your focus is on leveraging the most powerful forces at your disposal to make your initiative succeed.

It is useful to work in all four of the above frames to maximize your efforts. Work with the team to identify opportunities for action in each frame. Many actions exist in more than one frame, which is great—just put them somewhere.

Checklist for Framing Your Efforts

Next to the force field analysis diagram from Step 5, set up another large piece of paper and use it to collect team suggestions for to the following brainstorming exercises:

- Identify *driving* forces in your force field that can be *strengthened* by actions in each of the four frames.
- Identify *driving* forces that can be *added* to your force field by actions in each of the four frames.
- Identify *restraining* forces in your force field that can be *diminished* by actions in each of the four frames.
- Identify *restraining* forces that can be *removed* to your force field by actions in each of the four frames.
- Identify opportunities for flipping *restraining* forces into *driving* forces by actions in each of the four frames.

Let the ideas flow. In the next step, you will sort through and prioritize the ways you can best disturb your force field to meet your interests.

Here are some actions in each frame that our hypothetical school team identified as important to its change initiative.

Structural frame:

- Purchase creative math texts
- Schedule non-required math courses throughout the day
- Schedule shared prep periods for team teachers

- Recruit more interns
- Hire another math teacher

Human resources frame:

- Hire a math coach
- Provide in-service professional development on creativity in math
- Connect the high school math team to elementary teams
- Offer stipends for course development
- Inform guidance counselors of the change initiative

Symbolic frame:

- Create funny posters of math teachers
- Post math assignments to bulletin boards
- Deliver math-related presentations at school assemblies
- Ensure that math projects are visible around building
- Display enrollment data for non-required courses
- Place math rooms strategically in building
- Lobby for an article on the math program in your local newspaper
- Post student-created math videos online

Power and politics frame:

- Encourage popular students to enroll in non-required math classes
- Encourage popular students to create math-related videos and presentations

- Bring a local celebrity in to discuss a math-related issue

Step 7: Choose High-Impact Actions

As a mentor said to me once when my head was spinning from all the possibilities and limitations of running a school, "You can do *anything*, but you can't do *everything*." It's now time to cull through all the actions you brainstormed in Step 6. You can't do everything, so you must decide what you *will* do and regularly revisit these actions as the data you collect inform how you're progressing on each.

Begin by separating your potential actions into the following four categories:

1. High impact, low effort. These actions should rise to the top of your list. (Note that some actions will only provide a high impact over a long period of time of sustained low effort.)

2. High impact, high effort. One of the reasons to have a diverse team in place is that one's idea of "low effort" is another's idea of "high effort." The team may be able to distribute work on a given action so that efforts aren't a burden to any single individual.

3. Low impact, low effort. These types of actions are always worth keeping in the mix. Many may be clustered in the symbolic frame, including the innumerable daily actions of leadership, such as reminding the community of the initiative and inspiring all to persevere.

4. Low impact, high effort. These actions are far from the top of your priority list. If anyone on your team sees a confluence of unlikely circumstances that might lead an action to have a high impact, refer to the risk analysis in Step 1 and say something along these lines: "This action is not off the table. None of them are. For now, let's set it aside. Circumstances may unfold that bring us back to this consideration."

Not everyone will agree on where each action goes. Feel free to place a controversial action on the boundary between categories or to set it aside as too volatile to be easily defined. It is rare that a single action is critical to a shift in the force field. When categorizing actions, be sure to invoke positions and interests: "Our interest is to effectively disturb the force field; each action simply represents one way to do it. In the end we'll have enough actions to do it well."

It is important to separate the brainstorming process in Step 7 from the decision-making process, especially when emotions are running high. Take a 15-minute break and encourage participants to head back to their classrooms or offices and ponder the possibilities on their own.

When categorizing actions, our hypothetical school team chose to set two of them— connecting elementary with high school faculty and placing math rooms strategically around the building—aside because participants couldn't agree on their level of impact or effort. Here is how they categorized the other actions:

High impact, low effort:

- Change the definition of "required"
- Offer stipends for course development
- Persuade popular students to make videos/presentations
- Post student math videos online
- Deliver math-related presentations in assemblies
- Inform guidance counselors of the change initiative
- Display enrollment data for non-required courses

High impact, high effort:

- Schedule non-required math courses throughout the day
- Purchase creative math texts
- Schedule shared prep periods for team teachers
- Hire another math teacher
- Hire a math coach

Low impact, low effort:

- Provide in-service training on creativity in math
- Post funny posters of math teachers
- Create bulletin boards for math assignments
- Ensure that math projects are visible around building
- Persuade popular students to enroll in math classes
- Lobby for an article on the school's math program in the local newspaper

- Bring a local celebrity in to discuss a math-related topic

Low impact, high effort:

- Recruit more interns

Step 8: Decide Who Does What

Knowing who does what is integral to your school's culture. In an effectively run school, the vast majority of people know their roles and operate with a certain degree of autonomy, allowing the exchange of information, materials, and decisions to flow freely along well-worn routes. "How we do things around here" shouldn't be a mystery. One reason change can be hard is that, by definition, it shifts the meaning of "how we do things around here." Uncertainty about roles and responsibilities can breed confusion and ultimately derail your change initiative.

Most schools are not democracies: they contain defined hierarchies across which power is not evenly distributed. Leaders must manage the contradiction between democratic ideals and the reality of making decisions that affect a large group of professionals, parents, and staff who are wise, experienced, and capable of contributing to the change initiative. Although not everyone can, wants to, or should be in charge, everyone benefits from knowing how they are able to contribute. Members of the community need to know where they fit in the plan; without letting them know, you invite resistance.

The Six Steps of Articulating and Distributing Responsibilities

Transparency and a well-articulated distribution of responsibilities are indispensable. There are six steps leaders can use to apprise stakeholders of decisions related to the change initiative (Senge, 1994). Importantly, these steps need not be taken in sequence—they can be used in a variety of configurations depending on the needs of the initiative:

1. Tell. Leaders take on the responsibility of making decisions and mandating them to others. This step is efficient, at least in the short term, because all it requires from others is simple and uncreative compliance. *Example:* Leaders tell stakeholders, "There is a new state regulation in place that has very specific conditions with which we must comply."

2. Sell. Leaders articulate the benefits of decisions, including how they align with the shared interests and mission of the school, and supply background information to stakeholders. *Example:* Having decided to purchase a new alarm system, leaders remind the community of a recent break-in at the school and explain that the building will now be more secure each night.

3. Test. Leaders assume they have enough information for a test run of the change initiative, and they understand the importance of getting input from the community along the way. This step communicates the leadership's desire for feedback from stakeholders. *Example:* The leadership team develops a new attendance page on the website that teachers will test for one month, after which they will provide the team with their input.

4. Consult. Leaders need abundant input from the school community before they make any decision, and this step communicates as much. Communicate your needs to the community directly: "We have a decision to make. We absolutely need your ideas to do our best. We must include your thinking. Help us out." *Example:* The school must replace all the classroom furniture to meet new codes, so the leadership convenes a teacher group to determine priorities before making any purchases.

5. Collaborate. Leaders work with members of the community to develop and implement plans for change. This step often supports decisions that are fulfilled with creativity and a high level of commitment by those involved. *Example:* In developing new guidelines for recess, leaders ensure that every voice in the school counts equally.

6. Delegate. Leaders relinquish tight control over the change initiative in favor of building community and flexibility, making sure to convey the most important interests to be met and any specific guidelines for doing so. It is preferable for leaders to remain active in the change process to demonstrate their commitment. *Example:* Leaders delegate a team of teachers to develop and implement a plan for increased diversity at assemblies.

Here's an example of how the steps might work in one particular sequence:

- **Consult.** Leaders convene a consulting team to gather ideas for a plan.
- **Tell.** Leaders craft the plan and tell the team about it.
- **Sell.** Leaders sell the plan in an attempt to enlist volunteers to help implement the plan.
- **Delegate.** Leaders delegate certain responsibilities to volunteers.
- **Test.** Leaders announce that the plan is now operating in "test" mode.
- **Consult.** Leaders reconvene the consulting team to assess the results of the plan being tested.

Note that in this case, the "Consult" step appears twice, and the "Collaborate" step doesn't appear at all. That's OK—there are any number of configurations that can work, depending on the circumstances.

A reminder of the importance of the roles that leaders assign themselves: Because leaders manage the momentum for change and because their role in any school program carries such a huge symbolic weight and because they have the most authority in the school, it is essential that they demonstrate how they themselves will contribute to the change initiative. George Patton said it simply: "Do everything you ask of those you command." You have to roll up your sleeves and lead by example, not merely from a swivel chair.

The change team should examine the priority list from Step 7, this time answering the following questions:

1. Which action belongs in the Tell step, and how can we most effectively communicate its aims?

2. Which action belongs in the Sell step, and who among us would be best at doing the selling?

3. Which action should we run as a test? How long should the test last?

4. What role can members of the school community play in the Consult step? How much diversity of perspective can we build into a consulting team?

5. What opportunities exist for leaders to collaborate with members of the community?

6. Which actions will best serve both the initiative and community by being delegated to others? How will we support those to whom we delegate tasks?

Remember to stay focused on your interests—don't get bogged down in disagreements about any single action. It is your responsibility to help the community keep its eye on the mission.

Here is how our hypothetical leadership team might sequence the six steps for deciding who does what to support the change initiative:

1. Tell. The principal does all the telling to the community, communicating the vision of change and the fact that a math coach will be hired and stipends will be offered.

2. Sell. The principal sells the initiative to the math faculty, and the chair of the math department sells the plan to the rest of the staff.

3. Test. The principal and the leadership team develop changes to the schedule that they will test-run for one semester before reviewing their effectiveness.

4. Consult. The principal consults with the math team and the guidance counselors on changing definitions of "required" for course descriptions, identifying the prerequisites for the math coach position, developing in-service opportunities, selecting new text books, and expanding course offerings.

5. Collaborate. A subcommittee of the leadership team is created to focus on publicizing the initiative by way of posters, bulletin boards, videos, and assemblies.

6. Delegate. Leaders delegate the implementation of schedule changes to guidance staff.

Step 9: Put Together an Action Plan

It is now time to develop a comprehensive action plan, bearing in mind the six sub-steps of Step 8: Consider the structural, symbolic, and political reasons for crafting individuals' roles in the initiative. Remind the team that achieving the long-term vision of change will be an ongoing process, support the team by being well organized, and motivate the team by modeling your commitment to change and the positive vision of an improved school.

Because substantial change happens over a long period of time, every action plan requires a "reconvene" date at which time leaders can review data and stories and determine which tasks remain to be accomplished and which may need adjusting.

You must decide how to disseminate the action plan. When doing this, you are working in the human resource, symbolic, and political frames all at once. Support those who are doing the work, provide the community with a sense of purpose and determination, and rally your supporters and those whose influence is critical to success.

Remember to celebrate every positive accomplishment along the way as you implement your plan. What may have begun as the work of isolated bright spots might now reveal a more widespread pattern of practice. Start each meeting with stories of success. Check off tasks, both large and small, that have taken root. Share examples of how the vision is becoming steadily manifested in the life of the school. Celebrate!

The Action Plan Worksheet

Every change initiative should use an Action Plan Worksheet to keep track of and communicate important elements of the plan. Here is an example of a worksheet with the answers filled in to reflect the initiative of our hypothetical school:

1. Vision of change and main interests: We will have a universally praised, outstanding math program that inspires students, supports the role that teachers play in shaping our school, and helps make our school the pride of the community for what we accomplish as a team.

2. Current specific short-term goals:

- More students signing up for non-required math courses
- Higher scores on standardized tests
- More students contributing math projects to our academic fair

3. Current data to collect:

- Enrollment numbers for non-required math courses
- Number of students signing up for multiple math courses

- Survey data of prerequisite skills students think they need to sign up for math electives

Reconvene date: October 15

4: Specific Actions

- **Tell staff the vision:** *Who:* Principal. *Deadline:* By Sept. 7. *Resources needed:* Staff meeting.
- **Hire coach:** *Who:* Principal. *Deadline:* By Nov. 1. *Resources needed:* Grant application.
- **Secure stipends:** *Who:* Principal. *Deadline:* By Jan. 15.
- **Collect data:** *Who:* Leadership team. *Start & end dates:* Sept. 1–Jan. 15. *Resources needed:* Online survey program, school records.
- **Create schedule changes and inform guidance staff:** *Who:* Leadership team. *Deadline:* By Jan. 15.
- **Meet with math dept. to inform and consult:** *Who:* Principal. *Deadline:* Sept. 6.
- **Develop new math courses:** *Who:* Math team. *Deadline:* Jan. 15.
- **Begin publicity to boost math presence:** *Who:* Leadership team. *Deadline:* Oct. 12. *Resources needed:* Photographs, bulletin boards, graphic design contributions, video lab.

Step 10: Sustain the Change

Although we all like to cross items off our agendas, the steps necessary for implementing and sustaining are not easily crossed off. All of the good that happens in school can only be accomplished through continual attention. A time will come when your change initiative has taken root and become part of the school's culture—part of "how we do things around here."

Checklist for Sustaining Change

Use this checklist to assess the sustainability of your change initiative.

_____1. The change team continues to meet and produce updated action plans and is no longer dependent on a consultant or an official school administrator.

_____2. The team receives ongoing structural support through scheduling and resources.

_____3. The team disseminates evidence that the actions targeted in Step 3 are being accomplished.

_____4. The team reviews and periodically collects more of the data identified in Step 4.

_____5. The team identifies additional opportunities for collecting relevant data in the school community.

_____6. The composition of the team membership evolves, with new members bringing in fresh ideas and energy.

Here is how our hypothetical school might describe its change initiative a year into the process:

The math department chair is now heading the change initiative. To support the initiative, the school has budgeted an hour per month for meeting with a consultant and reduced the lunch-duty schedules of teachers on the team. The team continues to produce an action plan after each "reconvene" meeting, which it then shares with the school leadership. Periodically, the team shares its plans and accomplishments at staff meetings.

The data that the team has collected show a significant increase in the number of students who have signed up for non-required math courses for the following year. In an end-of-year report to school leadership, the team notes that scores on standardized tests cannot yet reflect the changes in progress and identifies when in the next testing cycle scores might be used as a marker. The team has also identified two interrelated new targets for action: increasing the number of students developing interdisciplinary projects related to math and inviting teachers from the art and physical education departments to join the change team. The team is developing a staff survey to determine how many opportunities currently exist in the school for students to conduct interdisciplinary projects, and intends to develop a force field and to use the four frames in acting on the data results.

To give your feedback on this publication and
be entered into a drawing for a free ASCD
Arias e-book, please visit
www.ascd.org/ariasfeedback

ascd | arias™

ENCORE

PITFALLS TO AVOID

When I was a principal, I came up with a marvelous idea to improve my school. I was so excited that I couldn't wait to take action, so the next morning I decided to charge forward.

Everything fell apart. I created a disaster that took weeks to fix.

The steps in these pages should prevent you from making the mistake of disturbing your force field without knowing enough about it and ensure that you move from inertia to action in the most effective manner. You don't have to account for every possible risk before initiating change, but you should have a realistic sense of potential pitfalls and of your capacity to manage the inevitable unexpected circumstances that you're bound to face.

If you find your initiative is stalled or in chaos, review each of the 10 steps to see if you skipped an item or need to repeat a step. Then, check your plan against the following categories of pitfalls.

Confusion. This can be the result of an incomplete vision of change and poorly defined driving interests. The team may need to further align its initiative with interests so that actions can build on one another. Without clarity on vision and interests, people will pull in random directions. *Recommended course of action:* Review and promote the vision for change, interests, and action plan. You may need to push up the "reconvene" date for the team's next meeting.

Interference. When people in the school community feel left out, misunderstood, or ignored, they will often try to upend a plan. Work in the political frame by empowering stakeholders who might win over skeptics through influence and bargaining. It's possible that those interfering with the plan may simply need to be heard, which might indicate poor communication. *Recommended course of action:* Review and develop your political support. Find a role for those who feel ignored, perhaps as consultants.

Apprehension. Many people approach change with dread, feeling incapable of carrying out the tasks assigned to them. They may also be prone to imagining worst-case scenarios that paralyze their ability to act. *Recommended course of action:* Review the team's risk-assessment and damage control capabilities, provide staff with more direction, advertise successes, and provide struggling team members with a partner.

Indifference. Many people in schools are already working very hard; they just lack incentives to work harder, or to shift their work to accommodate the change plan. Others may have seen previous change initiatives come and go to little effect. *Recommended course of action:* Provide staff with incentives for reaching short-term targets, advertise successes, and provide leadership opportunities to your most influential staff.

Frustration. Even your initiative's most ardent supporters can sometimes become frustrated with the process, often due to a lack of resources or feedback about their effectiveness. *Recommended course of action:* Push up the "reconvene" meeting to review resources, collect and organize your data to show the impact of supporters' efforts on the force field, and join more closely with those who are implementing the initiative at different levels.

References

Bolman, L., & Deal, T. (1984). *Reframing organizations: Artistry, choice, and leadership.* San Francisco: Jossey-Bass.

Fullan, M. (2001). Leading in a culture of change. San Francisco: Jossey-Bass.

Heath, C., & Heath, D. (2010). *Switch: How to change things when change is hard.* New York: Random House.

Senge, P. (1994). *The Fifth Discipline fieldbook: Strategies and tools for building a leadership organization.* New York: Doubleday.

About the Author

Jeffrey Benson has worked in nearly every school context in his almost 40 years of experience in education: as a teacher in elementary, middle, and high schools; as an instructor in undergraduate and graduate programs; and as an administrator in day and residential schools. He has studied and worked side by side with national leaders in the fields of special education, learning theory, trauma and addiction, school reform, adult development, and conflict resolution. He has been a consultant to public and private schools, mentored teachers and principals in varied school settings, and has written on many school-based issues. Jeffrey can be reached at his website, www.jeffreybenson.org.

Related ASCD Resources: School-Based Management

At the time of publication, the following ASCD resources were available (ASCD stock numbers appear in parentheses). For up-to-date information about ASCD resources, go to www.ascd.org.

ASCD EDge® Group
Exchange ideas and connect with other educators interested in school-based management on the social networking site ASCD EDge® at http://ascdedge.ascd.org/

Books

The Differentiated School: Making Revolutionary Changes in Teaching and Learning Carol Tomlinson, Kay Brimijoin, and Lane Narvaez (#105005)

Guiding School Improvement with Action Research Richard Sagor (#100047)

How to Solve Typical School Problems Nancy Ohle and Cindy Lakin Morley (#194175E4)

The New Principal's Fieldbook: Strategies for Success Pam Robbins and Harvey Alvy (#103019)

The Results Fieldbook: Practical Strategies from Dramatically Improved Schools Mike Schmoker (#101001)

School Culture Rewired: How to Define, Assess, and Transform It Steve Gruenert and Todd Whitaker (#115004)

The **WHOLE CHILD** Initiative helps schools and communities create learning environments that allow students to be healthy, safe, engaged, supported, and challenged. To learn more about other books and resources that relate to the whole child, visit www.wholechildeducation.org.

For more information: send e-mail to member@ascd.org; call 1-800-933-2723 or 703-578-9600, press 2; send a fax to 703-575-5400; or write to Information Services, ASCD, 1703 N. Beauregard St., Alexandria, VA 22311-1714 USA.

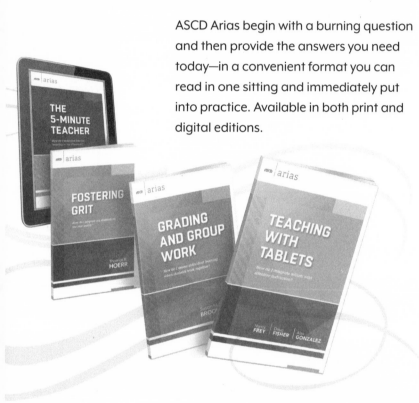